T0350554

Answer Book

Time

Measure

Shape, Position and Movement

Money and Finance

Information Handling

Heinemann

Part of Pearson

Contents

Time Pupil Book 5

Page 3
Time Problems

1. 2 hours 'example'
2. 4 hours
3. 3 hours
4. 4 hours
5. 3 hours
6. 5 hours

Rocket Answers will vary.

7. 8:00 'example'
8. 3:00
9. 10:30
10. 4:30

Page 4
Quarter past, quarter to

1. quarter past 2 'example'
2. quarter past 4
3. quarter to 9
4. quarter past 7
5. quarter to 6
6. quarter past 10

Rocket quarter past 2, quarter past 4, quarter to six, quarter past 7, quarter to 9, quarter past 10

7. quarter to 2 'example'
8. quarter past 12
9. quarter past 6
10. quarter to 12

Page 5
15 minutes

1. quarter to 3 'example'
2. quarter past 7
3. half past 8
4. 4 o'clock
5. half past 10
6. quarter past 2
7. 4:30 'example'
8. 7:00
9. 11:30
10. 11:00
11. 3:45
12. 9:45
13. 1:15
14. 9:00
15. 7:15

Rocket Three times

Page 6
5 minutes

1. 15 minutes 'example'
2. 45 minutes
3. 35 minutes
4. 40 minutes
5. 25 minutes
6. 35 minutes
7. 40 minutes

8. 10:40
9. 7:50

Rocket Answers will vary

Page 7
5 minutes

1. twenty-five past 6 'example'
2. quarter past 9
3. twenty to 2
4. twenty to 12
5. ten to 2
6. ten to 3

Rocket ten to 8, five past 11, 3 o'clock, five to 1, five to 3, ten to 5

7. 3:25 'example'
8. 5:05
9. 7:20
10. 6:50
11. 5:50
12. 4:30

Page 8
Minutes 'past' and 'to'

minutes past the hour
1. 21 'example'
2. 18
3. 27
4. 9
5. 32
6. 46
7. 25
8. 11

minutes to the hour
1. 39 'example'
2. 42
3. 33
4. 51
5. 28
6. 14
7. 35
8. 49

Rocket Answers will vary.

9. 10 minutes past 4
   quarter past 4
   19 minutes past 4
   26 minutes to 5
   20 minutes to 5
   quarter to 5
   11 minutes to 5

Page 9
Reading the time

minutes 'past' or 'to'
1. 27 minutes past 2 'example'
2. 16 minutes past 3
3. 8 minutes to 7
4. 19 minutes to 6
5. 28 minutes to 10

digital times
1. 2:27 'example'
2. 3:16
3. 6:52

4. 5:41
5. 9:32
6. 7:55 'example'
7. 8:04
8. 10:12
9. 5:55
10. 10:30
11. 3:52

Rocket Answers will vary.

Page 10
am and pm

1. 7:20 am 'example'
2. 8:50 pm
3. 11:35 am
4. 5:45 pm
5. 3:45 pm
6. 1:15 am
7. 8:22 am

Rocket Answers will vary.

8. 6:00 am 'example'
9. 1:45 pm
10. 8:10 pm
11. 12:20 am

Page 11
Timetables

1. 11:10
2. Monday, Tuesday, Wednesday, Thursday
3. 5 times
4. Art, English, RME and PE/Music
5. The first lesson every day: English and Maths
6. Longest: the first lesson every day: English and Maths
   Shortest: the second lesson every day: Maths, History/Geography, Science and Drama
7. 8 hours 15 minutes

Rocket Answers will vary.

8. 2 hours 10 minutes
9. bowling
10. 30 minutes
11. The film

Page 12
Timetables

1.

Moon	Mars	Jupiter
7:15 am	11:00 am	1:00 pm
9:00 am	12:20 pm	3:40 pm
3:00 pm	7:00 pm	10:00 pm
6:00 pm	12:00 midnight	7:25 am

2. The 9:00 am rocket
3. 7:00 pm
4. 12:00 midnight
5. The 6:00 pm rocket
6. Answers will vary.

Page 13
Timetables

1.

Entrance	Zebras	Monkeys	Lions	Penguins
9:30	9:40	9:50	10:00	10:10
10:20	10:30	10:40	10:50	11:00
12:15	12:25	12:35	12:45	12:55
2:45	2:55	3:05	3:15	3:25
4:05	4:15	4:25	4:35	4:45

2. Answers will vary. The following table is one possibility.

Feed tigers	Clean tigers	Give vitamins	Provide straw	Shut tigers in
7:00 am	8:00 am	10:00 am	1:00 pm	
3:00 pm	4:00 pm	5:00 pm		6:00 pm

Page 14
Timetables

1. 1:30 pm
2. The 2:30 pm train
3. 1 hour
4. 2 hours 20 minutes
5. The 1:30 pm train
6. 3 hours 30 minutes
Rocket 8:40 am train: 12 noon
 11:40 am train: 3:00 pm
 1:30 pm train: 5:10 pm
7. getting up 20 minutes
 eating breakfast 20 minutes
 cleaning teeth 5 minutes
 packing bags 20 minutes
 walking to station 40 minutes
Rocket Answers will vary

Time PPMs
PPM 170
Yesterday, today, tomorrow

1. Lines joining 'yesterday' to the first picture 'example', 'today' to the second picture, 'tomorrow' to the third picture.
2. A line joining 'tomorrow' to the third picture, 'yesterday' to the first picture and 'today' to the middle picture.
3. Answers will vary.

PPM 171
Past, present or future?

1. future 'example', past, present past, present, future future, present, past
2. Pictures will vary.

PPM 172
When do I usually do this?

Answers may vary but are most likely to be:
1. morning 'example'
2. night
3. evening
4. afternoon or evening
5. evening
6. morning or afternoon
7. morning or afternoon
8. morning or evening

PPM 173
Months

1. Answers will vary.

PPM 174
Time all around us

1. ✗ 'example'
2. ✓
3. ✗
4. ✗
5. ✓
6. ✗
7. ✓
8. ✗
9. ✓
10. ✓
11. ✗
12. ✓
3, 4, 9 and 12 circled

PPM 175
When in the year?

1. January
2. December
3. October
4. April
5. August
6. November
7. Answers will vary but could include: June, July or August
8. Answers will vary but could include: December, January or February

9. Answers will vary but could include: September, October or November
10. Answers will vary but could include: March, April or May
11. Answers will vary.

PPM 176
Days

1. Friday 'example'
2. Tuesday
3. Wednesday
4. Sunday
5. Monday
6. Saturday
7. Thursday
8. Monday, Tuesday, Wednesday, Thursday, Friday, Saturday, Sunday

PPM 177
Months of the year

1. January, February, March, April, May, June, July, August, September, October, November, December
2. December, January, February
3. June, July, August
4. January

PPM 178
Calendars

1. Friday 'example'
2. Thursday
3. Tuesday
4. Sunday
5. Saturday
6. Saturday
7. 15th
8. 5th

5

PPM 179

The month of June

1–7.

Monday	Tuesday	Wednesday	Thursday	Friday	Saturday	Sunday
		1 Swimming	2	3	4	5
6	7	8 Swimming	9	10 Staying at Nanna's	11 Staying at Nanna's	12 Staying at Nanna's
13 School play	14 School play	15 Swimming	16	17	18	19 Sally's birthday
20	21 Sports Day 'example'	22	23	24 Break up!	25	26
27	28	29	30 Go on holiday			

Time PPMs

PM 180

Days and weeks

1. January
   10 days
   1 week and 3 days

   February
   8 days
   1 week and 1 day

   March
   22 days
   3 weeks and 1 day

   April
   15 days
   2 weeks and 1 day

PPM 181

At the theme park

1. hour 'example'
2. minutes
3. minutes
4. seconds
5. minutes
6. minutes
7. seconds
8. hours

PPM 182

More or less (1)

1. less 'example'
2–9. Answers will vary.
   Children can check their own answers using a second hand on a clock, or by counting.

PPM 183

More or less (2)

1. more 'example'
2–8. Answers will vary. Children should check their own answers using a minute timer.

PPM 184

Who takes longer?

1. quarter of an hour 'example'
2. half a minute
3. one hour
4. 2 minutes
5. 5 minutes
6. 40 seconds
7. 1 day
8–10. Answers will vary.

PPM 185

Units of time

1.	12 'example'		
2.	52	3. 7	4. 24
5.	60	6. 60	7. 2
8.	104	9. 21	10. 10
11.	Answers will vary.		
12.	Answers will vary.		

PPM 186

Which unit?

1. seconds 'example'
2. minutes
3. seconds or minutes
4. years
5. hours
6. minutes
7. months or years
8. minutes or hours

PPM 187

Clock faces (o'clock and half past)

1.

'example'

2. The clock hands should point to eleven o'clock
3. The clock hands should point to half past twelve
4. The clock hands should point to half past nine
5. The clock hands should point to eight o'clock
6. The clock hands should point to half past two
7. The clock hands should point to one o'clock
8. The clock hands should point to half past five
9. The clock hand should point to half past ten

PPM 188

Digital times (o'clock and half past)

1. 4:00 'example'
2. 11:00
3. 12:30
4. 9:30
5. 8:00
6. 2:30
7. 1:00
8. 5:30
9. 10:30

PPM 189

O'clock

1. The answer should show 5:00 in the digital clock. 'example'
2. The answer should show 8:00 in a digital clock.
3. The answer should show hands pointing to ten o'clock on an analogue clock.
4. The answer should show hands pointing to six o'clock on an analogue clock.
5. The answer should show 3:00 in a digital clock.
6. The answer should show 11:00 in a digital clock.
7. The answer should show hands pointing to nine o'clock on an analogue clock.
8. The answer should show 1:00 in a digital clock below.

PPM 190
Half past

1. 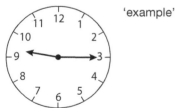 'example'

2. The answer should show 8:30 in a digital clock.
3. The answer should show hands pointing to half past twelve on an analogue clock.
4. The answer should show hands pointing to half past three on an analogue clock.
5. The answer should show 9:30 in a digital clock.
6. The answer should show 2:30 in a digital clock.
7. The answer should show hands pointing to half past one on an analogue clock.
8. The answer should show hands pointing to half past ten on an analogue clock.

PPM 191
Feeding times

1. 4 hours 'example'
2. 5 hours
3. 2 and a half hours
4. Answers will vary.

PPM 192
Clock faces (quarter past, quarter to)

1. 'example'

2. The answer should show hands pointing to quarter past eight.
3. The answer should show hands pointing to quarter past eleven.
4. The answer should show hands pointing to quarter past ten.
5. The answer should show hands pointing to quarter past five.
6. The answer should show hands pointing to quarter to four.
7. The answer should show hands pointing to quarter to one.
8. The answer should show hands pointing to quarter to twelve.
9. The answer should show hands pointing to quarter past three.

PPM 193
Clock hands

1. 'example'

2. The answer should show hands pointing to quarter past seven.
3. The answer should show hands pointing to quarter to three.
4. The answer should show hands pointing to quarter to six.
5. The answer should show hands pointing to quarter past four.
6. The answer should show hands pointing to quarter to four.
7. The answer should show hands pointing to quarter past ten.
8. The answer should show hands pointing to quarter to eight.
9. The answer should show hands pointing to quarter past six.
10. The answer should show hands pointing to quarter to nine.
11. The answer should show hands pointing to quarter past nine.
12. The answer should show hands pointing to quarter to twelve.

PPM 194
Digital times (quarter past, quarter to)

1. 3:15 'example'
2. 6:45
3. 12:15
4. 9:15
5. 7:45
6. 10:45
7. 12:45
8. 5:15
9. 11:45

PPM 195
Analogue and digital

1. 'example'

2. The answer should show 7:15 in a digital clock.
3. The answer should show hands pointing to quarter past ten on an analogue clock.
4. The answer should show hands pointing to quarter to seven on an analogue clock.
5. The answer should show 3:45 in a digital clock.
6. The answer should show 1:15 in a digital clock.
7. The answer should show hands pointing to quarter to ten on an analogue clock.
8. The answer should show hands pointing to 11:45 in a digital clock.

PPM 196
Minutes

1. 20 minutes 'example'
2. 10 minutes
3. 15 minutes
4. 45 minutes
5. 25 minutes
6. 40 minutes
7. 55 minutes
8. 35 minutes

PPM 197
Five minutes

1. 8:00 'example'
2. 8:05
3. 8:10
4. 8:15
5. 8:20
6. 8:25
7. 8:30
8. 8:35
9. 8:40
10. 8:45
11. 8:50
12. 8:55

PPM 198
Timetable

1. 7 minutes 'example'
2. 19 minutes
3. 55 minutes
4. 34 minutes
5. 14 minutes
6. 40 minutes
7. 46 minutes
8. 41 minutes
9. Answers will vary.

Measure Pupil Book 5

Page 15
Which unit?

1. kilometres 'example'
2. centimetres
3. grams
4. litres
5. metres
6. millimetres
7. millilitres
8. kilograms

Rocket Answers will vary.

Page 16
Metres and centimetres

1–4. Answers will vary.
Rocket Answers will vary.

Page 17
Units of length

1. metres 'example'
2. centimetres
3. centimetres
4. metres
5. kilometres
6. centimetres
7. millimetres
8. metres

Rocket Answers will vary.

Page 18
Centimetres

1. 5 cm 'example'
2. 3 cm   **3.** 8 cm   **4.** 4 cm
5. 7 cm   **6.** 6 cm   **7.** 5 cm
8. 8 cm   **9.** 10 cm   **10.** 9 cm
Rocket Answers will vary.

Page 19
Measuring length

1–9. Answers will vary.
Rocket Answers will vary.

Page 20
Grams and kilograms

1–8. Answers will vary.
9. 10 'example'
10. 2   **11.** 5   **12.** 20
13. 100   **14.** 4

Page 21
Weight

1. C 'example'
2. H   **3.** F   **4.** B
5. G   **6.** A   **7.** I
8. D   **9.** E
Rocket   1.   2900 g
            2.   2400 g
            3.   4400 g
            4.   700 g
            5.   9600 g
            6.   1300 g
            7.   6800 g
            8.   4600 g
            9.   2300 g

Page 22
Litres and millilitres

1. less 'example'
2. more   **3.** equal
4. less   **5.** less
6. less
Rocket
1. 200 ml less   **2.** 200 ml more
3. equal   **4.** 800 ml less
5. 500 ml less   **6.** 750 ml less
7. five   **8.** two
9. four   **10.** 1000 ml
11. 3000 ml   **12.** 5000 ml
13. 500 ml

Page 23
Scales

1. 800 ml 'example'
2. 300 ml   **3.** 500 ml
4. 700 ml   **5.** 200 ml
6. 900 ml   **7.** 400 ml
8. 600 ml   **9.** 1400 ml
10. 1800 ml   **11.** 700 ml

12. 1100 ml
Rocket 200 ml and 1800 ml
         600 ml and 1400 ml
         900 ml and 1100 ml

Page 24
Area

1. area is 5 squares 'example'
2. area is 9 squares
3. area is 6 squares
Rocket Answers will vary.
4. area is 14 tiles 'example'
5. area is 22 tiles
6. area is 28 tiles
7. Answers will vary.

Page 25
Area

1. 5 squares   **2.** 7 squares
3. 9 squares   **4.** 13 squares
Rocket Answers will vary.
5. 12 squares   **6.** 9 squares
7. 12 squares   **8.** 10 squares
9. 7 squares   **10.** 13 squares
11. Drawings will vary.

Page 26
Area

1. a and f
   area = 8 sq cm 'example'
   b and g
   area = 7 sq cm
   c and e
   area = $5\frac{1}{2}$ sq cm
2. d has no partner.
   Drawings will vary but should have
   an area of $7\frac{1}{2}$ sq cm
3. a = 7 sq cm 'example'
   b = 5 sq cm
   c = $6\frac{1}{2}$ sq cm
   d = $4\frac{1}{2}$ sq cm
Rocket Answers will vary.

Page 27
Solving problems

1. 6 cm 'example'
2. 34 cm   **3.** 10 cm
4. 26 cm   **5.** 40 cm
6. 50 cm
7–10. Answers will vary.

Page 28
Measurement problems

1. ruler 'example'
2. ruler or tape measure
3. measuring jug
4. scales
5. scales
6. measuring jug
7. tape measure

8. metre stick
Rocket   1.   cm or mm
            2.   mm
            3.   ml
            4.   kg or g
            5.   kg or g
            6.   ml
            7.   cm
            8.   m

Page 29
Problems

1. true   **2.** true
3. false   **4.** true
5. 24 jugfuls 'example'
6. 10 cupfuls   **7.** 3600 ml
8. 100 tablespoons
9. 60 ml   **10.** 4 tins
Rocket Answers will vary.

Page 30
Measurement problems

1. A 400 ml 'example'
   B 42 ml
   C 45 ml
   D 340 ml
2. 3 ml
3. 827 ml
4. 90 ml
5. 50 ml
6. 442 ml 558
Rocket Answers will vary.

Page 31
Problems

1. 20 plums   **2.** 5 kg
3. 1 kg   **4.** 8 tins
5. True 'example'
6. False   **7.** False
8. False
Rocket Answers will vary.

Measure PPMs

PPM 199
Length, weight, capacity

1. length 'example'
2. capacity   **3.** weight
4. length   **5.** capacity
6. length   **7.** weight
8. capacity   **9.** length
10. weight

PPM 200
Longer, taller, wider, heavier

1. 4 paces
2. 30 centimetres
3. 25 kilograms
4. 6 metres
5. 400 grams
6. 220 grams

PPM 201
Length
1–6. Answers will vary.

PPM 202
Measuring length
1–7. Answers will vary.

PPM 203
The same as an apple
1–4. Answers will vary.

PPM 204
Weight
1–7. Answers will vary.

PPM 205
Cupfuls
1–4. Answers will vary.

PPM 206
Measuring capacities

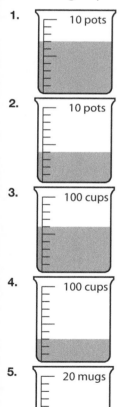

1.
2.
3.
4.
5.
6.

PPM 207
Capacity
1–7. Answers will vary.

PPM 208
Area

1. Doormat
2. Piece of toast
3. Chopping board
4–5. Answers will vary.

PPM 209
Measuring area

1. 13 squares
2. 12 squares
3. 15 squares
4. 21 squares
5. 9 squares
6. 20 squares
7. 12 squares
8. 25 squares
9. 18 squares
10. Shape with 9 squares
11. Shape with 25 squares

PPM 210
Standard units

1. cross 'example'
2. cross
3. tick
4. cross
5. tick
6. tick
7. tick
8. cross
9. tick
10. cross
11. tick
12. cross

PPM 211
Units

1. metres 'example'
2. litres
3. kilograms
4. centimetres
5. kilometres
6. Answers will vary.

PPM 212
Measuring length

1.

line	guess	measure	difference
Annie	Answers will vary	8 cm	Answers will vary
Baz	Answers will vary	3 cm	Answers will vary
Colin	Answers will vary	4 cm	Answers will vary
Devdas	Answers will vary	7 cm	Answers will vary
Erin	Answers will vary	10 cm	Answers will vary

2. Answers will vary.

PPM 213
Length
1–7. Answers will vary.

PPM 214
Grams
1–6. Answers will vary.

PPM 215
Grams and kilograms

1. 10 g
2. 500 g
3. 500 g
4. 600 kg
5. 1 kg
6. 1 kg
7. 30 g
8. 3 kg
9. 70 g

PPM 216
Weighing
1–4. Answers will vary.

PPM 217
Reading scales

1. 0 kg 400 g
2. 0 kg 700 g
3. 0 kg 900 g
4. 1 kg 600 g
5. 2 kg 500 g
6. 3 kg 500 g

PPM 218
One litre

1. more than 'example'
2. less than one litre
3. less than one litre
4. more than one litre
5. more than one litre
6. less than one litre
7 and 8. Answers will vary.

PPM 219
Scales

1. Children's colouring should show just over 1 litre. 'example'
2. Children's colouring should show about 2 litres.
3. Children's colouring should show nearly 5 litres.
4. Children's colouring should show just less than 6 litres.
5. Children's colouring should show just over 3 litres.
6. Children's colouring should show about half a litre.
7. Children's colouring should show 3 and a bit litres.
8. Children's colouring should show about 6 litres.
9. Children's colouring should show just under 4 litres.
10. Bucket 3

PPM 220
Perimeter and area

1.

Shape	A	B	C	D	E	F	G	H	I
Perimeter in cm	8 'example'	12	16	12	16	12	14	16	12
Area in sq cm	4 'example'	5	15	9	7	8	6	7	5

PPM 221
Estimating

1. 'example' 50 g
2. 25 m
3. 100 l
4. 18 cm
5. 400 g
6. 400 ml
7. 200 cm
8. 60 g
9. Answers will vary.

Shape, Position and Movement Pupil Book 6

Page 3
3D objects

1. a, d, 'example' e, h
2. f, k, l
3. g, i, m
4. b, j
5. a, b, d, e, f, g, h, i, j, k, l, m
6. b, c, g, i, j, m
Rocket circle: b, c, g, i, j, m
square: a, d, e, f, h, k, l

2. 2 cubes 'example'
   3 cuboids
   1 pyramid
   1 cone
   1 cylinder
   6 prisms
   1 sphere
Rocket (a) 2 faces 1 vertex 1 edge
(b) 1 face 0 vertices 0 edges
(c) 6 faces 8 vertices 12 edges
(d) 3 faces 0 vertices 2 edges
(e) 6 faces 8 vertices 12 edges
(f) 5 faces 5 vertices 8 edges
(g) 6 faces 8 vertices 12 edges
(h) 6 faces 8 vertices 12 edges
(i) 6 faces 8 vertices 12 edges

Page 4
3D objects

1. b, d, 'example', h, j
2. a, e, g, i, k
3. b, d, h, j,
4. a, g, i, k
Rocket pyramid (square-based)

Page 5
3D objects

1. (a) cone
   (b) sphere
   (c) cube
   (d) cylinder
   (e) cuboid
   (f) pyramid
   (g) cuboid
   (h) cube
   (i) cuboid

Page 6
Flat and curved faces

1. a, d, 'example' e, g, h, i
2. j
3. b, c, f
4. j
5. none
6. a, d, e, g, h, i
7. a, e, g
8. b, c, f, j
9. i, d
Rocket Answers will vary.

Page 7
Sides

1. (a) 3 'example'
   (b) 4
   (c) 5
   (d) 3
   (e) 6
   (f) 5
   (g) 4
   (h) 4
   (i) 4
   (j) 8
   (k) 7
   (l) 3
   (m) 6
   (n) 5
2. triangles: a, d, l; pentagons: c, f; hexagons: e, m
Rocket Answers will vary.

Page 8
2D shapes

1 and **2.** Answers will vary.
Rocket Answers will vary.

Page 9
Joining shapes

1. b, c, d
2. f, g, h
3. Answers will vary.
   For example, equilateral triangles, squares and equilateral triangles.
Rocket Answers will vary.

Page 10
Tiling templates

1–6. Answers will vary.
Rocket Answers will vary.

Page 11
Symmetry

1. Yes 'example'
2. No
3. Yes
4. No
5. No
6. Yes
7. Yes 'example'
8. Yes
9. No
10. No
11. Yes
12. Yes
Rocket Answers will vary.

Page 12
Symmetrical patterns

1.   'example'

2.

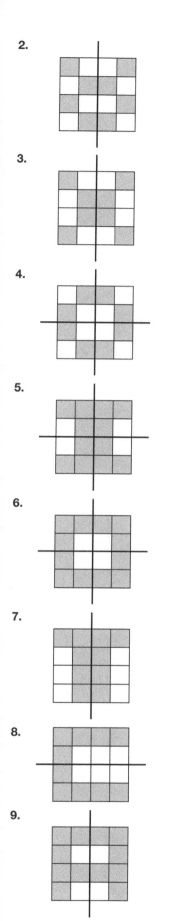

3.

4.

5.

6.

7.

8.

9.

Rocket Answers will vary.

Page 13
Symmetry

1. Yes 'example'
2. No   **3.** Yes   **4.** No
5. No   **6.** Yes

7.

   'example'

8.

9.

10.

11.

12.

Rocket Answers will vary.

Page 14
Position

1. C2 'example'
2. D4   **3.** E2
4. D1   **5.** B1
6. A4   **7.** D2
8. D3   **9.** A1
10. Mrs Sums   **11.** Mr Keen
12. Mrs Winnett   **13.** Flopsy
14. Mrs Cotter   **15.** Mrs Grim

Rocket Answers will vary.

Page 15
Position

1. A5 'example'
2. D1   **3.** E1
4. E3   **5.** D5
6. C5   **7.** A1
8. B1   **9.** barn
10. house   **11.** goats

12. river   **13.** trees
14. flowers
15. hedgehogs, goats, otters

Rocket Answers will vary.

Page 16
Position

1. E3 'example'
2. B5   **3.** E1   **4.** F5
5. A2   **6.** C1   **7.** C4
8. D6
9.

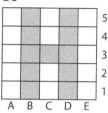

10.

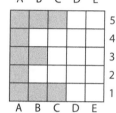

11.

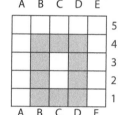

Page 17
Making turns

1. computer 'example'
2. fish tank   **3.** TV
4. computer   **5.** fish tank
6. bed   **7.** computer

Rocket Answers will vary.

Page 18
Routes

1. m 'example'
2. b   **3.** m   **4.** y

Rocket Answers will vary.

Page 19
Cube models

1. 6 'example'
2. 6   **3.** 8   **4.** 8
5. 12   **6.** 12   **7.** 10

Rocket Answers will vary.

Page 20
Quadrilaterals

1. Yes 'example'
2. Yes   **3.** Yes
4. No   **5.** No

11

6. Yes
7. No
8. Yes
9. No
10. 4 and 7 are pentagons,
    5 is a hexagon
11. Answers will vary.
Rocket Answers will vary.

Page 21
Shape properties

1. quadrilateral
2. hexagon
3. hexagon
4. pentagon
5. quadrilateral
6. octagon
7. pentagon
8. quadrilateral
9. heptagon
10. 3, 5, 6
11. 1, 2, 3, 4, 5, 6, 7, 8
12. 5
Rocket Answers will vary.

Page 22
Names of shapes

1. True   2. True   3. True
4. False   5. True   6. False
Rocket Answers will vary.
7. (a) pentagon 'example'
   (b) triangle
   (c) octagon
   (d) hexagon
   (e) quadrilateral or rectangle
   (f) triangle
   (g) hexagon
Rocket Answers will vary.

Page 23
Prisms

1. 5 rectangles, 2 pentagons
   'example'
2. 4 rectangles, 2 quadrilaterals
3. 4 rectangles, 2 squares
4. 6 rectangles, 2 hexagons
5. 8 rectangles, 2 octagons
6. 3 rectangles, 2 triangles
7.

Prism	Faces
Triangular prism	5
Quadrilateral prism	6
Pentagonal prism	7
Hexagonal prism	8
Heptagonal prism	9
Octagonal prism	10

8. The number of faces on a prism is
   the number of sides on the end-
   face + 2 (e.g. a triangular prism has
   a 3-sided end-face and 5 faces).
Rocket 10 sides

Page 24
3D objects

1.

shape	b	f or d	d or f	a	c	e
faces	4	5	5	6	7	8

shape	b	f	d	a	c	e
edges	6	8	9	12	15	18

shape	b	f	d	a	c	e
vertices	4	5	6	8	10	12

Rocket The shapes with a vertex where
more than 3 edges meet is f.

Page 25
3D objects

1. True 'example'
2. False
3. True — it has some triangular faces
   but may have another
   shape for the base
4. True   5. True
6. True   7. False
8. False — it could have some square
   faces
9. False   10. False
Rocket Answers will vary.
11. Answers will vary.

Page 26
Symmetry

1.
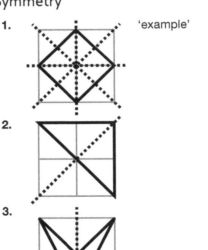
'example'

2.
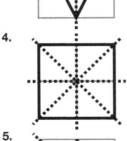

3.

4.

5.

6.
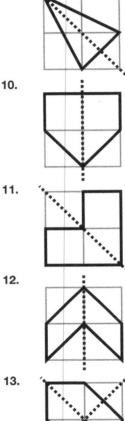

7.

8.

9.

10.

11.
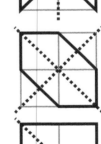

12.

13.

14.

15.

16.

17. 'C' has 1 line of symmetry
'L' has no lines of symmetry
'A' has 1 line of symmetry
'I' has 2 lines of symmetry
'R' has no lines of symmetry
'E' has 1 line of symmetry

18. Answers will vary.

Page 27
Lines of symmetry

1. 3   'example'

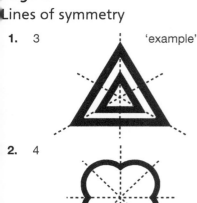

2. 4

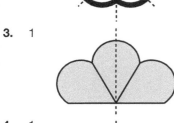

3. 1

4. 1

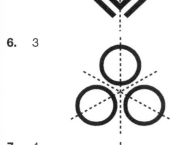

5. 2

6. 3

7. 4

8. 1

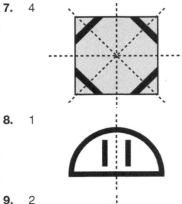

9. 2

10. Answers will vary.
Rocket Answers will vary.

Page 28
Lines of symmetry

1. Answers will vary.

2.

	no lines of symmetry	1 line of symmetry	2 lines of symmetry	3 lines of symmetry	more than 3 lines of symmetry
A			✓		
B	✓				
C					✓
D		✓			
E		✓			
F		✓			
G		✓			
H	Answers will vary.				
I	Answers will vary.				

Page 29
North, South, East, West

1. West 'example'
2. East   **3.** South
4. East   **5.** South
6. North   **7.** West
8. South
9. East, West, North, West, North, South, East, North
Rocket Answers will vary.

Page 30
North, South, East, West

1. East 'example'
2. South   **3.** West
4. West   **5.** East
6. South   **7.** East
8. North   **9.** West
10. East, South 'example'
11. West, North
Rocket Answers will vary.

Page 31
North, South, East, West

1. 'example'

2.   **3.**

4.   **5.**

6.   **7.**

8.   **9.**

10.   **11.**

Rocket Answers will vary.

Page 32
Right angles

1. 1 right angle 'example'
2. 2 right angles
3. 3 right angles
4. 1 right angle
5. 2 right angles
6. 1 right angle
7. 3 right angles
8. 1 right angle
9. 2 right angles
10. 3 right angles
Rocket Answers will vary.

Page 33
Turning

1. 6 'example'
2. 3   **3.** 3   **4.** 9
5. 10   **6.** 1
Rocket 3 right-angle turns in the opposite direction or 5 right-angle turns in the same direction
7. True   **8.** False
9. True   **10.** True

Page 34
Turning

1. Ghost Train 'example'
2. Wall of Death
3. Wall of Death
4. Wall of Death
5. Ghost Train
6. Big Dipper
7. Wall of Death
8. Ghost Train
9. Rick: anticlockwise, 1 right angle
Liz: clockwise, 3 right angles
Kevi: anticlockwise, 2 right angles
Pam: clockwise, 4 right angles
Rocket Answers will vary.

Page 35
Right angle turns

1. 1 rt ang c
2. 1 rt ang antic
3. 1 rt ang c
4. 1 rt ang antic
5. 1 rt ang c
6. 1 rt ang c
7. 1 rt ang antic
8. 1 rt ang antic
9. 1 rt ang c
10. 1 rt ang antic
11. 1 rt ang antic
12. 1 rt ang c
13. 1 rt ang c
14. 1 rt ang antic
15. 1 rt ang antic
16. 1 rt ang antic
17. 1 rt ang c
18. 1 rt ang c

Rocket Answers will vary.
Note that children's 'shorthand' will vary. Also angles can be described in different ways, e.g. turning clockwise through 3 right angles has the same result as turning anticlockwise through 1 right angle.

Page 36
Turning

1. 2 right angles 'example'
2. 3 right angles
3. 1 right angle
4. 3 right angles
5. 1 right angle
6. 2 right angles
7. 1 right angle
8. 4 right angles

9–12. Answers will vary.
Rocket Answers will vary.

Page 37
Angles

1. less than 'example'
2. more than
3. equal to
4. equal to
5. more than
6. less than
7. less than
8. equal to
9. more than
10. equal to
11. more than
12. less than

Rocket Answers will vary.

Page 38
Shape angles

1. 3 'example'
2. 1
3. 4
4. 1
5. 2
6. 0
7. 1
8. 0
9. 2
10. 3
11. 1
12. 8

Rocket Answers will vary.
For example,

14

Page 39
Giving directions

1–6. Answers will vary.
Rocket Answers will vary.

Shape, Position and Movement PPMs

PPM 222
3D models

1–5. Answers will vary. Expect children to justify their reasoning.

PPM 223
2D pictures

1–3. Answers will vary.

PPM 224
Shape patterns

1–6. Answers will vary.

PPM 225
Describing 3D objects

Answers will vary.

PPM 226
Comparing 3D objects

1–9. Answers will vary. Expect children to explain and justify their answers.

PPM 227
Sides

1. 2 sides i, e
   3 sides j, h
   4 sides 'example' a, f, c
   5 sides k, d
   6 sides l, g, b
2. Answers will vary.

PPM 228
Making 2D shapes

1. 5, 'example'
2. 8
3. 6
4. 4
5. 5
6. 6
7. 5
8. 8
9. 4
10–12. Answers will vary.

PPM 229
Printing shapes

1. circle and long thin rectangle
2. square
3. 'example' square and triangle
4. square and rectangle
5. triangle and rectangle
6. rectangle and long thin rectangle
7. Answers will vary.

PPM 230
Investigating symmetry

1.

2.

3.

4.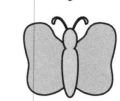

5.

6.

7.

8.

PPM 231

House

1.

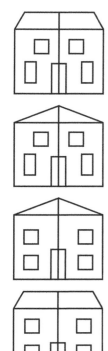

2. Answers will vary.

PPM 232

Symmetry

1.

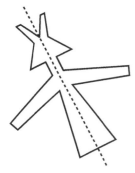

2.

3.

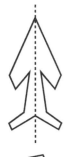

4.

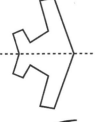

5.

6.

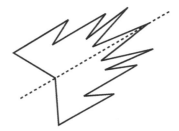

7. Answers will vary.

PPM 233

Above, below, beside, left, right

1. left of 5 – a line to 4 'example'
above 14 – a line to 8
above 9 – a line to 3
left of 18 – a line to 17
below 6 – a line to 12
above 30 – a line to 24
right of 22 – a line to 23
right of 32 – a line to 33
left of 35 – a line to 34
below 20 – a line to 26
below 13 – a line to 19
above 21 – a line to 15

2. Answers will vary.

PPM 234

Up, down, left, right

1. c 'example'
2. b **3.** l
4. a **5.** y
6. h **7.** q
8. u **9.** b
10. t
11 and **12.** Answers will vary.

PPM 235

Where?

1.

2. Answers will vary.

PPM 236

Routes

1. 3
2–4. Answers will vary.

PPM 237

Routes

1 and **2.** Answers will vary.

PPM 238

Letters

1. i 'example'
2. o
3. n
4. h
5. Answers will vary.

PPM 239

3D objects

1. a cone on a cylinder
2. a pyramid on a cuboid
3. a pyramid on a cube 'example'
4. a sphere on a cone
5. a sphere on a cylinder
6. a cube on a cuboid
7. a cone on a cone
8. a pyramid on a pyramid
9. Answers will vary.

PPM 240

Sorting mistakes

1. The cone and the triangular prism are incorrectly placed.

has a square face   is a prism

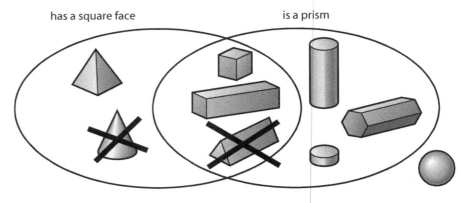

2. The cone is incorrectly placed.

has a triangular face   has more than 5 corners

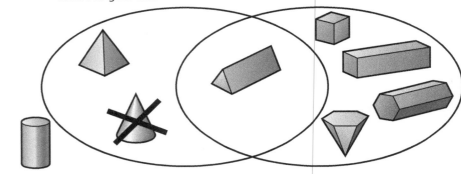

PPM 241

Pentagons and hexagons

1.
   pentagon   'example'

2.
   hexagon

3.
   pentagon

4.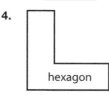
   hexagon

5.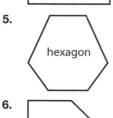
   hexagon

6.
   pentagon

7. Answers will vary.

PPM 242

Names of shapes

1. rectangle 'example'
2. triangle   3. octagon   4. pentagon   5. square
6. hexagon   7. triangle   8. pentagon   9. hexagon

PPM 243

Sorting mistakes

1. The rectangle is incorrectly placed.

has fewer than 5 sides   has sides all the same length

2. The triangle and the pentagon are incorrectly placed.

has 4 corners   has more than 4 sides

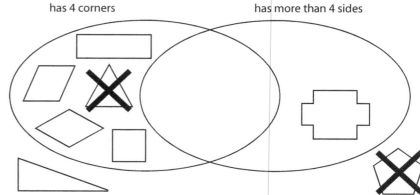

3. Answers will vary.

16

PPM 244
Faces

1. 2 squares 4 rectangles 'example'
2. 2 hexagons 6 rectangles
3. 2 triangles 3 rectangles
4. 6 rectangles
5. 6 squares
6. 1 square 4 triangles

PPM 245
Tiling

1 and 2. Answers will vary.

PPM 246
Shape patterns

1 and 2. Answers will vary.

PPM 247
Symmetry

1.

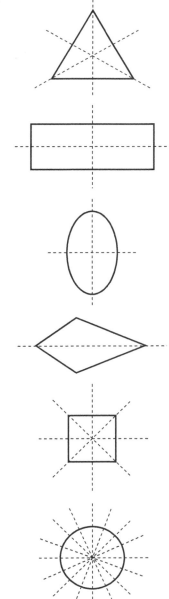

2. a, b, c, e, f.

PPM 248
Symmetry

1.

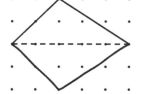
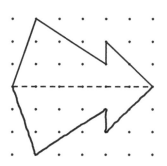
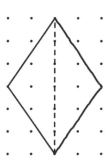
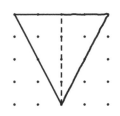
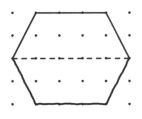
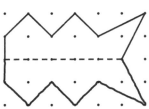
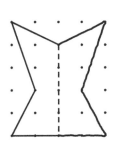

2. Answers will vary.

PPM 249
Symmetrical shapes

1.

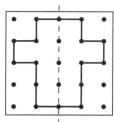

2.

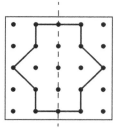

3.

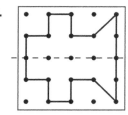

4–9. Answers will vary.

PPM 250
Position

1–8.

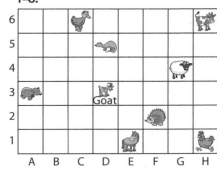

9. Otter
10. Cow
11. Badger

PPM 251
Clockwise and anticlockwise

1. a 'example'
2. c
3. c
4. a
5. a
6. c
7. c
8. a
9. c
10. a
11. c
12. a

PPM 252

Movement in a maze

Answers will vary.

PPM 253

Symmetry

1. 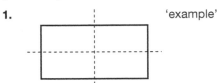 'example'

2.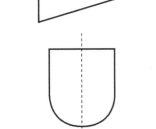

3.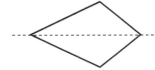

4.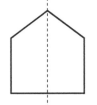

5.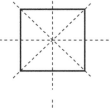

6.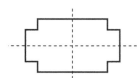

7.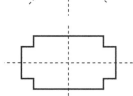

8. There are no lines of symmetry.

PPM 254

North, South, East and West

1. E 'example'
2. S
3. S
4. E
5. S
6. E
7. N
8. W
9. N
10. W
11. N
12. W

PPM 255

Turning

1. 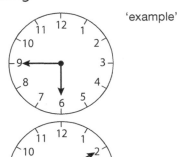 'example'

2.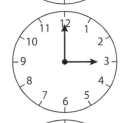

3. (clock image)

4.

5. (clock image)

6.

7.

8.

PPM 256

Right angles

The angles will be coloured:
1. yellow
2. green
3. blue
4. green
5. yellow
6. yellow
7. yellow
8. blue
9. yellow

PPM 257

Right angles

1. A, D, G, H, I, L
2. Answers will vary.

PPM 258

North, South, East and West

No answers required.

PPM 259

North, South, East and West

1. East 2, South 2, West 3, South 2 'example'
2. East 4, North 2, East 2, South 6
3. North 4, West 4, South 5, East 6, North 3
4. East 2, North 4, East 2, South 2, East 2, North 4
5. West 3, North 2, West 1, South 4, East 6, North 3
6. Answers will vary.

Shape, Position and Movement APM

PPM 591

Letter symmetry

0 lines of symmetry:
F, G, J, L, N, P, Q, R, S, Z

1 line of symmetry:
A, B, C, D, E, K, M, T, U, V, W, Y

2 lines of symmetry: H, I, O, X

Money and Finance Pupil Book 7

Page 3

Same values

1. £1·00 'example'
2. 10p 3. 10p 4. £1·00
5. 50p 6. 25p 7. 9p
8. 25p 9. 50p 10. 9p
Rocket Purses 1 and 4; 2 and 3; 6 and 8; 5 and 9; 7 and 10

Page 4
Totals

1. £15 'example'
2. £8 **3.** £60 **4.** £3
5. £1·24 'example'
6. £3·16 **7.** £4·05 **8.** £1·55
9. £2·21 **10.** £6·15

Rocket £1·01, £1·02, £1·05, £1·10,
£1·20, £1·50, £2·00, £3·00;
£2·01, £2·02, £2·05, £2·10,
£2·20, £2·50, £3·00, £4·00.

Page 5
How much?

1. 31p 'example'
2. 54p **3.** 85p **4.** 29p
5. 50p **6.** 25p
7. Any coins with a total of 58p.

Page 6
Fewest coins

1. 5p and 2p 'example'
2. 10p and 2p
3. 20p and 5p
4. 50p, 10p, 5p and 1p
5. 50p, 20p, 10p, 5p and 2p
6. £1 and 50p
7. £1, 10p and 5p
8. £2, £1 and 1p
9. £2, £1, 50p, 20p, 10p, 5p, 2p and 1p

Rocket Answers will vary.

Page 7
True or false?

1. true 'example'
2. true
3. false
4. true
5. true

Rocket Answers will vary.

Page 8
Which is cheaper?

1. a by 35p 'example'
2. a by 3p
3. b by 13p
4. b by 15p
5. a by 13p
6. a by 25p
7. b by 45p
8. a by £1·01

Rocket £1·59 (£1·99–40p)

Page 9
Can I afford it?

1. no 'example'
2. no **3.** no **4.** yes
5. yes **6.** no

Rocket Answers will vary.

Page 10
Prices

1. £4·99, £5·05, £6·25, £8·04, £8·40,
£9·49, £9·99, £11·99, £12·50
2. any three amounts between £8·40
and £12·50
3. two

Rocket Answers will vary.

Page 11
Which coin or note?

1. £2 coin 'example'
2. £5 note **3.** 50p coin
4. £1 coin **5.** £5 note
6. £10 note **7.** £5 note
8. £1 coin **9.** £20 note

Rocket ice cream, tomatoes, ice lolly,
magazine, pot plant.

Page 12
Can I afford them?

1. yes 'example'
2. no **3.** yes **4.** yes
5. no **6.** yes

Rocket 5p, 1p, 3p, 57p.

Page 13
Money problems

1. Answers will vary.
2. 85p: 1 × 50p; 1 × 20p; 1 × 10p;
1 × 5p
39p: 1 × 20p; 1 × 10p; 1 × 5p; 2 × 2p
13p: 1 × 10p; 1 × 2p; 1 × 1p
54p: 1 × 50p; 2 × 2p
76p: 1 × 50p; 1 × 20p; 1 × 5p; 1 × 1p
62p: 1 × 50p; 1 × 10p; 1 × 2p
95p: 1 × 50p; 2 × 20p; 1 × 5p
44p: 2 × 20p; 2 × 2p
28p: 1 × 20p; 1 × 5p; 1 × 2p; 1 × 1p
67p: 1 × 50p; 1 × 10p; 1 × 5p; 1 × 2p
3. Answers will vary. The most is
£2·00 (four 50p coins), the least is
20p (four 5p coins).

Rocket Answers will vary.

Page 14
Money problems

1. example 70p + 30p = £1·00
5p + 6p = 11p
£1·00 + 11p = £1·11
2. 40p + 20p = 60p
7p + 5p = 12p
60p + 12p = 72p
3. 60p + 10p = 70p
5p + 7p = 12p
70p + 12p = 82p
4. 70p + 40p = £1·10
8p + 5p = 13p
£1·10 + 13p = £1·23
5. 70p + 50p = £1·20
5p + 8p = 13p
£1·20 + 13p = £1·33

6. 70p + 50p = £1·20
4p + 6p = 10p
£1·20 + 10p = £1·30
7. 80p + 70p = £1·50
4p + 5p = 9p
£1·50 + 9p = £1·59
8. £1·30 + 60p = £1·90
5p + 1p = 6p
£1·90 + 6p = £1·96
9. £1·20 + 30p = £1·50
£1·50 + 4p = £1·54
10. £1·23 **11.** £1·66
12. £1·38 **13.** £1·46
14. £1·51 **15.** £1·25
16. £2·34 **17.** £2·41

Rocket Answers will vary.
The prices should be anywhere
from 72p to 99p, e.g. 72p and
99p, or 74p and 97p, or 84p
and 87p.

Page 15
How much for one?

1. 23p 'example'
2. 22p **3.** 55p **4.** 31p
5. 42p **6.** 75p

Rocket Answers will vary but children
should find they need to make
the total price a multiple of 5p.

Page 16
Sharing

1. 20p 'example'
2. 30p **3.** 22p **4.** 18p
5. 50p **6.** £2·10 **7.** £1·20
8. £1·03

Rocket Answers will vary.

Page 17
Special offers

1. 80p 'example'
2. £1·45 **3.** £1·55 **4.** 38p
5. 20p 'example'
6. £1 **7.** 60p **8.** 80p

Rocket Answers will vary.

Page 18
Ticket prices

1. £18 **2.** £20 **3.** £48
4. £49 **5.** £53

Rocket Answers will vary.

Page 19
Special offers

1. £18 + £9 = £27 'example'
2. £3·20 + £1·60 = £4·80
3. £25 + £12·50 = £37·50
4. £5·90 + £2·45 = £8·85
5. £2·80 + £1·40 = £4·20
6. £4·20 + £2·10 = £6·30

7. £7·20 + £3·60 = £10·80
8. £36 + £18 = £54
Rocket Answers will vary.

Money and Finance PPMs

PPM 260
Ways to pay

1. tick 'example'
2. cross
3. tick
4. tick
5. tick
6. cross
7. cross
8. tick
Answers will vary.

PPM 261
Getting money

1–6. Answers will vary.

PPM 262
Coins

1. Silver: 5p, 10p, 20p, 50p
   Brown: 1p, 2p
   Round: 1p, 2p, 5p, 10p, £1, £2
   Has corners: 20p, 50p
   More than 10p: 20p, 50p, £1, £2
   Less than 20p: 1p, 2p, 5p, 10p
2. Heaviest coin: answers will vary
3. Lightest coin: answers will vary

PPM 263
How much?

1. £260
2. £2·95
3. 38p
4. £5
5. £150
6. 15p
7. £400
8. £17
Answers will vary.

PPM 264
Coins

1. 20p ticked 2p crossed
2. £1 ticked 1p crossed
3. £2 ticked 1p crossed
4. £2 ticked 2p crossed
5. £1 ticked 5p crossed
6. 20p ticked 1p crossed
7. £2, £1, 50p, 20p, 10p, 5p, 2p, 1p or the reverse.

PPM 265
Totals

1. 52p 'example'
2. 21p
3. 53p
4. 17p
5. 90p
6. 23p
7. 75p
8. 31p
9. Tick purse 5 (90p).

PPM 266
Totals

1. £1·50
2. £1·40
3. £1·40
4. £2
5. £1·35
6. Check that shaded coins in each set total £1.

PPM 267
Coins

1 and 2. Answers will vary.

PPM 268
Fewest coins

1. Circle 50p, 20p and 10p coins
2. Circle 20p and 5p coins
3. Circle 50p and 5p coins
4. Circle 50p, 10p and 5p coins
5. Circle 20p, 20p and 5p coins
6. Circle 20p, 10p and 5p coins
7. Answers will vary.

PPM 269
Fewest coins

1. 10p, 2p, 1p 'example'
2. 10p, 5p, 1p
3. 20p, 10p, 5p
4. 20p, 20p, 2p
5. 10p, 5p, 2p, 2p
6. 20p, 5p, 2p
7. 50p, 2p, 1p
8. 50p, 10p, 5p, 2p
9. 50p, 20p, 5p, 2p, 1p
10. 50p, 20p, 10p, 1p
11. 20p, 10p, 5p, 2p, 1p
12. 20p, 20p, 5p, 2p, 2p

PPM 270
Coins

1–6. Answers will vary.

PPM 271
Money problems

	£2	£1	50p	20p	10p	5p	2p	1p	Total coins
68p			1		1	1	1	1	5
95p			1	2		1			4
£1·21		1		1				1	3
£2·40	1			2					3
£1·64		1	1		1		2		5
85p			1	1	1	1			4
£1·07		1				1	1		3
£3·60	1	1	1		1				4
£3·17	1	1			1	1	1	1	5

PPM 272
Can he afford it?

1. tick the CD and computer game
2. £5·75
3. tick the toffees and the magazine
4. £3·76
5. Answers will vary.

PPM 273
Change

1. felt-tipped pen: 4p
   flower: 18p
   eraser: 12p
   ball: 1p
2. flower
3. yoyo: 33p
   present: 26p
   pen: 12p
   sweet: 42p
4. sweet
5. frog: 44p
   box: 18p
   crayon: 73p
   cake: 87p
6. cake

PPM 274
Money problems

1. 58p
2. 32p
3. 13p
4. 16p
5. 60p
6. 25p
7. 17p

PPM 275
Money problems

1. 60p
2. 20p
3. 30p
4. 55p
5. 36p
6. 43p
7. 85p
8. 42p

PPM 276
Which to use?

1. 5p, 2p, 1
2. £1 and 20p
3. 20p and 20p
4. 50p, 50p, 20p, 20p, 20p
5. £20 note
6. £5, £1, 20p
7. no change, 80p, 14p, 10p, 25p, 13p

PM 277

hange

1. 19p 'example'
2. 4p
3. 92p
4. 82p
5. Answers will vary.

PM 278

eceipts

1. total cost £1·61 change given £3·39
2. total cost 79p change given 21p
3. total cost £1·35 change given 65p
4. total cost £1·69 change given £3·31
5. total cost £4·95 change given £5·05
6. total cost £4·70 change given £15·30
7. Answers will vary.

PM 279

alf price

1. 17p 'example'
2. 28p 3. 36p 4. 14p
5. 21p 6. 48p 7. 63p
8. £1·29

PM 280

uying several

1. 2 × 8p = 16p 'example'
2. 5 × 9p = 45p
3. 3 × 7p = 21p
4. 6 × 8p = 48p
5. 3 × 6p = 18p
6. 4 × 9p = 36p
1. 84p   2. 55p
3. 79p   4. 52p
5. 82p   6. 64p

PM 281

uying several

1. 2 × 41p = 82p 'example'
2. 4 × 22p = 88p
3. 3 × 45p = £1·35
4. 5 × 41p = £2·05
5. 2 × 63p = £1·26
6. 5 × 22p = £1·10
1. £4·18   2. £4·12
3. £3·65   4. £2·95
5. £3·74   6. £4·90

PM 282

Money problems

1. £16 'example'
2. £32   3. £1·20
4. £75   5. 96p
6. £240   7. £365·16

Information Handling Pupil Book 7

Page 20
Block graphs

1. 4 'example'
2. 3   3. 2   4. 5
5. 8   6. 7   7. 7
8. 9   9. 14   10. 10

Rocket Answers will vary.

Page 21
Pictograms

1. 2 'example'
2. 4   3. 6   4. 5
5. 8   6. 9   7. 17

Rocket Strawberry: £2
Vanilla: £2·50
Total: £8·50

Page 22
Pictograms

1. Children's pictograms should show:
   red row   4 boats
   yellow row   3 boats
   blue row   2 boats
   orange row   5 boats

Rocket Answers will vary.

Page 23
Venn diagrams

1
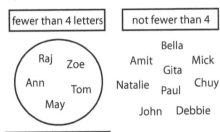

2. Answers will vary.

Rocket Answers will vary.

Page 24
Carroll diagrams

1.

	Joining word	Not joining word
Short word (fewer than 4 letters)	but and	cat dog
Not short word (4 or more letters)	where because which	chair table

2. Answers will vary.

Rocket Answers will vary but could be
Column: Electronic toy,
          Not electronic toy;
Row: Small, Not small.

Page 25
Carroll and Venn diagrams

1.

	2 syllables or fewer	Not 2 syllables
Words rhyming with sea	tree free wispy bee	blustery cheerfully summery
Words not rhyming with sea	autumn sun wasp spring wind	beautiful imagining

2.
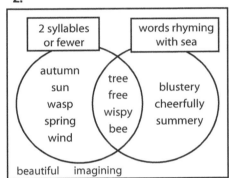

Rocket Answers will vary.

Page 26
Carroll and Venn diagrams

1.

	Animals with fur/hair	Animals without fur/hair
Pets	rabbit gerbil *cat*	goldfish stick insect lizard *spider*
Not Pets	kangaroo koala *lion*	*crocodile*

2. Answers will vary; examples above.

3.

	Multiples of 3	Not multiples of 3
Odd	21 27 33 39 45	23 25 29 31 35 37 41 43 47 49
Not odd	24 30 36 42 48	22 26 28 32 34 38 40 44 46

Rocket Sorting by multiples of any even number will make the first section empty.

Page 27
Always, sometimes, never

1. never true 'example'
2. always true
3. always true
4. sometimes true
5. never true
6. sometimes true
7. sometimes true
8. always true

Rocket Answers will vary.

Page 28
Likelihood

Some answers will depend on circumstance and children's opinion.

1. unlikely 'example'
2. certain or likely
3. likely or unlikely
4. impossible
5. likely or unlikely
6. likely or unlikely
7. unlikely or impossible
8. unlikely or likely
9–11. Answers will vary.

Page 29
Likelihood

Most answers will depend on circumstance and children's opinion.

1. likely 'example'
2. likely or unlikely
3. likely or unlikely
4. likely or unlikely
5. likely or unlikely
6. likely or unlikely
7. impossible
8. likely or unlikely
9. likely or unlikely
10. likely or unlikely

Rocket Answers will vary.

Page 30
Likelihood

Some answers will depend on circumstance and children's opinion. Typical answers are shown here.

likely	unlikely	impossible
2 3 5	4	1

always	sometimes	never
6 9	7 8	10 11

Rocket Answers will vary.

22

Page 31
Pictograms

1. 6
2. semi-detached house
3. 22
4. 28

Rocket Answers will vary.

Page 32
Pictograms

1. 6
2. 8
3. 8
4. green
5. yellow, purple and white
6. red
7. 28

Rocket Answers will vary.
For example, the number of passengers in a car.

Page 33
Pictograms

1.

| CD player | mobile phone | television | video player | DVD player | portable music player |

2. 8
3. 2

Rocket Answers will vary. For example, computer or radio.

Page 34
Bar graphs

1. Fantasy adventures
2. Historical stories
3. Stories about everyday life
4. 12   5. 4   6. 10

Rocket 1 vote: 32 children; 2 votes; 16 children.

Page 35
Bar graphs

1. 54
2. Cinderella and Robin Hood
3. Snow White
4. Beauty and the Beast
5. 40
6. 40

Rocket Answers will vary.

Page 36
Questionnaires

Answers will vary.

Page 37
Questionnaires

1 and 2. Answers will vary.

Page 38
Displaying information

1–4. Answers will vary.
Rocket Answers will vary.

Page 39
Charts

1–3. Answers will vary.

Information Handling PPMs

PPM 283
Recording
1–5. Answers will vary.

PPM 284
Information
1–5. Answers will vary.

PPM 285
Information
1–5. Answers will vary.

PPM 286
Carroll diagrams
1–3. Answers will vary.

PPM 287
Venn diagrams
1–3. Answers will vary.

PPM 288
Venn diagrams
1. They are multiples of 5.
2. Odd numbers in the ring, even numbers outside.
3. Answers will vary.

PPM 289
Tables
1–4. Answers will vary.

PPM 290
Questions
1 and 2. Answers will vary.

PPM 291
Tables
1–6. Answers will vary.

PPM 292
Tally chart
1.

Transport	Tallies	Total
skateboard	JHT	5
bicycle	JHT IIII	9
tricycle	JHT II	7
scooter	JHT I	6
roller blades	IIII	4

2. 31
3. Bicycle
4. Roller blades

PPM 293
Block graph
1 and 2. Answers will vary.

PPM 294
Block graph
1 and 2. Answers will vary.

PPM 295
Venn diagrams

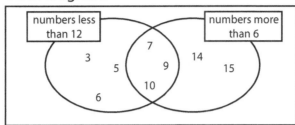

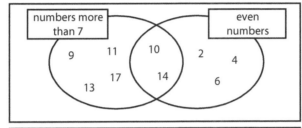

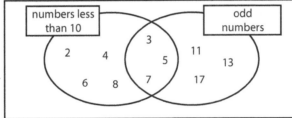

PPM 296
Tree diagram
1. Box 1: 1, 3, 5, 7, 9, 11, 13, 15, 17, 19
   Box 2: 2, 4, 6, 8, 10, 12, 14, 16, 18
   Box 3: 21, 23, 25, 27, 29, 31, 33, 35, 37, 39
   Box 4: 20, 22, 24, 26, 28, 30, 32, 34, 36, 38, 40
2. Box 1: 24, 28
   Box 2: 21, 22, 23, 25, 26, 27, 29, 30
   Box 3: 4, 8, 12, 16, 20
   Box 4: 1, 2, 3, 5, 6, 7, 9, 10, 11, 13, 14, 15, 17, 18, 19
3. Answers will vary.

PPM 297
Pictogram
1. green   2. blue   3. red
4. yellow   5. green   6. blue
7. red   8. blue   9. blue
10. green   11. 24

PPM 298
Pictogram
1. 10   2. 17   3. 15
4. 6   5. 16   6. 32
7. 15   8. 21   9. 14

PPM 299
Recording
1 and 2. Answers will vary.

PPM 300
Displaying information
1.

Vowel	Tallies
a	JHT JHT JHT JHT JHT
e	JHT JHT JHT JHT I
i	JHT I
o	JHT
u	JHT I

2.

Vowel	Frequency
a	25
e	21
i	6
o	5
u	6

3. Answers will vary.

Part of Pearson

Author Team: Lynda Keith, Hilary Koll and Steve Mills

Heinemann is an imprint of Pearson Education Limited, a company incorporated in England and Wales, having its registered office at Edinburgh Gate, Harlow, Essex, CM20 2JE. Registered company number: 872828

www.pearsonschools.co.uk

Heinemann is a registered trademark of Pearson Education Limited

Text © Pearson Education Limited 2011

First published 2011

18
10 9 8 7

British Library Cataloguing in Publication Data
A catalogue record for this book is available from the British Library

ISBN 978 0 435 047566

Typeset by Tech-Set Ltd, Gateshead
Cover design by Pearson Education Limited
Cover illustration Volker Beisler © Pearson Education Limited
Printed in the UK by Ashford Colour Press Ltd.

Acknowledgements
Every effort has been made to contact copyright holders of material reproduced in this book.
Any omissions will be rectified in subsequent printings if notice is given to the publishers.